PAPER
MANIA

Crafts, Activities, Facts, and Fun!

by Amanda Formaro

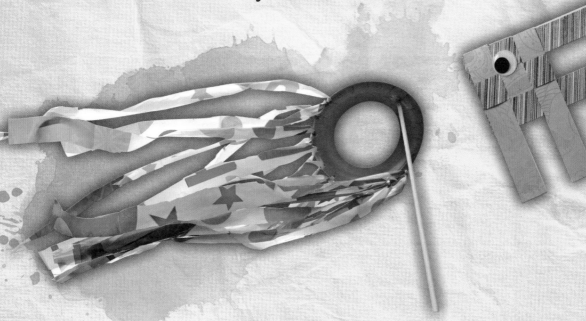

studio BOOKS

White Plains, New York • Montréal, Quebec • Bath, United Kingdom

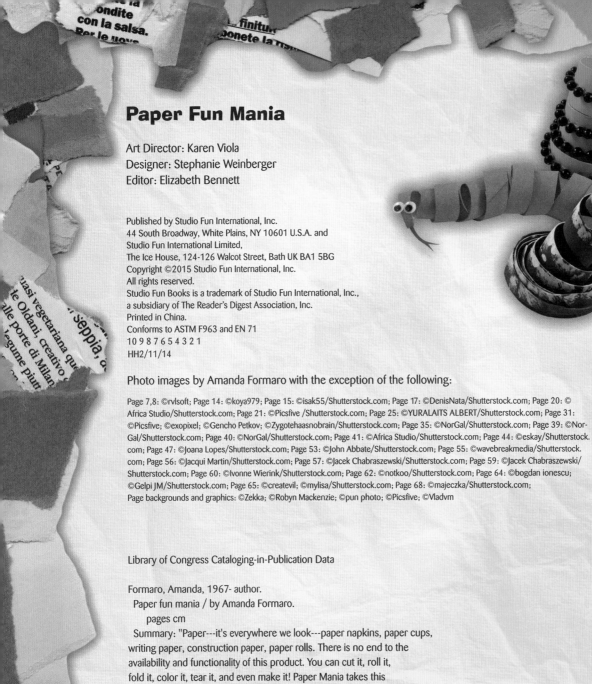

Paper Fun Mania

Art Director: Karen Viola
Designer: Stephanie Weinberger
Editor: Elizabeth Bennett

Published by Studio Fun International, Inc.
44 South Broadway, White Plains, NY 10601 U.S.A. and
Studio Fun International Limited,
The Ice House, 124-126 Walcot Street, Bath UK BA1 5BG
Copyright ©2015 Studio Fun International, Inc.
All rights reserved.
Studio Fun Books is a trademark of Studio Fun International, Inc.,
a subsidiary of The Reader's Digest Association, Inc.
Printed in China.
Conforms to ASTM F963 and EN 71
10 9 8 7 6 5 4 3 2 1
HH2/11/14

Photo images by Amanda Formaro with the exception of the following:

Page 7,8: ©rvlsoft; Page 14: ©koya979; Page 15: ©isak55/Shutterstock.com; Page 17: ©DenisNata/Shutterstock.com; Page 20: © Africa Studio/Shutterstock.com; Page 21: ©Picsfive /Shutterstock.com; Page 25: ©YURALAITS ALBERT/Shutterstock.com; Page 31: ©Picsfive; ©exopixel; ©Gencho Petkov; ©Zygotehaasnobrain/Shutterstock.com; Page 35: ©NorGal/Shutterstock.com; Page 39: ©Nor-Gal/Shutterstock.com; Page 40: ©NorGal/Shutterstock.com; Page 41: ©Africa Studio/Shutterstock.com; Page 44: ©eskay/Shutterstock.com; Page 47: ©Joana Lopes/Shutterstock.com; Page 53: ©John Abbate/Shutterstock.com; Page 55: ©wavebreakmedia/Shutterstock.com; Page 56: ©Jacqui Martin/Shutterstock.com; Page 57: ©Jacek Chabraszewski/Shutterstock.com; Page 59: ©Jacek Chabraszewski/Shutterstock.com; Page 60: ©Ivonne Wierink/Shutterstock.com; Page 62: ©notkoo/Shutterstock.com; Page 64: ©bogdan ionescu; ©Gelpi JM/Shutterstock.com; Page 65: ©createvil; ©mylisa/Shutterstock.com; Page 68: ©majeczka/Shutterstock.com;
Page backgrounds and graphics: ©Zekka; ©Robyn Mackenzie; ©pun photo; ©Picsfive; ©Vladvm

Library of Congress Cataloging-in-Publication Data

Formaro, Amanda, 1967- author.
  Paper fun mania / by Amanda Formaro.
      pages cm
  Summary: "Paper---it's everywhere we look---paper napkins, paper cups,
writing paper, construction paper, paper rolls. There is no end to the
availability and functionality of this product. You can cut it, roll it,
fold it, color it, tear it, and even make it! Paper Mania takes this
ubiquitous material and makes it fun and exciting! Filled with craft
projects, trivia, experiments, recycling projects, and more, this craft
book provides hours of creative fun!"-- Provided by publisher.
  Audience: Ages 6-10.
  ISBN 978-0-7944-3338-3 (alk. paper)
1. Paper work--Juvenile literature. 2. Handicraft--Juvenile
literature. I. Title.
  TT870.F655 2014
  745.54--dc23
                        2014031220

CONTENTS

Wanna hear a joke about paper?
Never mind, it's **TEAR**-able!

Paper. It's everywhere we look—writing paper, construction paper, tissue paper, newspaper, paper napkins, paper towels, the cardboard tube inside your paper towels—once you start looking you will be surprised by how much paper is around you. And there is so much you can do with paper. You can cut it, tear it, fold it, roll it, twirl it, color it, and paste it.

This book is packed with simple, creative (and most of all, fun) ways to make great stuff out of...you guessed it... paper! We'll show you how to make jewelry, toys, puppets, decorations, books, costumes—even your own paper! Along the way, you will learn some wacky facts and tear-ific tips about the humble piece of paper.

So let's tear in and get started! We guarantee that *Paper Mania* will make a paper maniac out of you!

No skills? No sweat! This symbol marks our simplest projects.

Crafting Rock Star? This symbol marks our harder projects.

Careful! This symbol marks the steps that require adult supervision for safety.

STUFF TO PASTE

Pasting Basics

PAPER MACHE

A combination of torn paper and paste, paper mache is great for making masks, animal figures, and sculptures. It's a bit messy (but that's what makes it fun!), so make sure to protect your clothing and your work surface!

Paste Recipe

All you need is flour and water to make this simple paste.

½ cup flour
1 cup water

Add half of the water to the flour and use a fork to stir to remove the lumps. Add small amounts of water until you reach a consistency similar to thin pancake batter.

Boiled Paste Recipe

This recipe takes a little more time, but boiling the mixture makes it last longer and it dries more clear than the simple paste.

1 cup flour
5 cups water
Medium saucepan

Pour four of the five cups of water into the saucepan and bring to a boil over medium-high heat. In a medium bowl, whisk together the flour and remaining cup of water until there are no more lumps. When the water is boiling, slowly add the flour and water mixture to the pan and whisk it together to make a smooth paste. Boil for 2-3 minutes, stirring frequently. Remove from heat and allow it to cool completely. Additional water can be added to thin the mixture if needed.

How to Paper Mache

Tear newspaper or other soft paper into strips. Dip newspaper into paste and run through your fingers to squeeze off the excess. Press the damp newspaper onto your surface. Continue this process, creating one full layer of coverage. Allow the first layer to dry completely before applying the next layer. Add 3-4 layers for a strong bond. Allow to dry completely (overnight is best) before decorating.

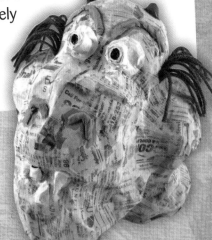

DECOUPAGE

Decorating objects such as boxes and jars with cut or torn pieces of paper is known as decoupage. First paint on a layer of glue, then add paper, then cover with one more layer of glue. The glue will dry hard and shiny. Once you start decoupaging, you will be amazed at the number of things you can decorate!

How to Decoupage

Cut or tear paper into pieces. Use a sponge applicator or a paintbrush to apply a thin coat of decoupage glue onto your surface. Place paper onto the sticky surface and paint over the edges of the paper to make sure it sticks. When entire surface is covered, paint a final generous coat of decoupage glue over the entire project.

Homemade Decoupage Glue

For kids' craft projects, homemade decoupage glue does the job and is less expensive. It's great for temporary projects, but if you think you will keep the item for many years, stick with store-bought decoupage glue; it will last longer over time.

1 part water
2 parts white craft glue

Mix the glue and water together and store in an airtight container.

STICKY TIPS

Here are some more types of glue you will find handy for some of the projects in this book.

✓ Glue sticks—excellent for attaching paper to paper with no lumps or bumps!

✓ White craft glue and school glue—perfect for adding textured items to paper, such as yarn, pom-poms, and cotton balls.

✓ Glue dots—No mess and super strong, glue dots are perfect for paper-to-paper projects. Peel one side of the plastic backing away, press the paper to the dot, lift the paper and the dot off the backing, and press the dot to the paper you are attaching.

CLIP TIPS

✓ Be sure to keep your brushes clean by rinsing them thoroughly in water as soon as you are done. If the glue dries on your brush it can be very difficult to remove and you may have to throw the brush away.

✓ If glue has gummed up inside the cap, remove it, rinse it in hot water, and use a toothpick to poke out dried glue that may be blocking the opening.

✓ For containers with screw-top lids, wipe away any glue drips from the threads as well as the inside of the cap before closing.

✓ Be sure to keep the lids or caps on your glue containers to keep them from drying out.

Decoupage Picture Frame

What You Need:
- ✓ Wooden frame
- ✓ Book pages
- ✓ Decoupage glue (see page 7)
- ✓ Sponge applicator

1 Remove glass and backing from the frame and set aside.

Don't toss your old, damaged books. Instead, recycle the pages by making cool frames—one for you and one for a friend! Use a picture book, an atlas, a dictionary, or any book you like.

2 Trace the frame onto the back of the book page you would like to use (we are using an old atlas).

3 Cut out the frame shape from the book page.

4 Apply a thin coat of decoupage glue to the back of the frame-shaped book page.

6 Apply a coat of decoupage glue over the entire surface.

7 When the glue is dry, you can put the glass back in the frame and add a photo!

5 Line up the book page over the frame and press in place, using your fingers to smooth.

Magazine Collage Art

An old magazine is all you need to inspire some creative masterpieces. Just add your imagination!

1 Look for a few colorful pages from old magazines.

2 Sketch a design onto a piece of white paper. It can be as simple or complicated as you want.

3 Cut shapes out of the magazine pages to fill in areas on your design.

4 Use a glue stick to apply the magazine pieces to the white paper.

5 You can use crayons and/or markers to add details to your art (flower stems, birds, etc).

What You Need:

- ✓ Construction paper
- ✓ White paper
- ✓ Glue stick
- ✓ Large googly eye (optional)
- ✓ White craft glue (optional)

Construction Paper Mosaic

You don't need expensive tiles to create beautiful mosaic art! Several colors of construction paper and a basic drawing are all you will need. So break out the glue stick and get busy creating!

1 Tear or cut construction paper into squares and small pieces.

2 Use a glue stick to draw the outline of your design on white paper (we made a fish). Press construction paper squares to the glue. Leave a small amount of space between each piece of paper.

3 Fill the entire piece of white paper with construction paper squares to complete your design, using different colors for different areas.

4 If you are making an animal, use white craft glue to attach a googly eye.

Decoupage Luminary

Don't toss out those empty jars! Save a few to make these colorful luminaries, great for lighting up the backyard for fun summer nights. PS: They also make great gifts!

What You Need:
✔ Recycled glass jars, labels removed
✔ Tissue paper
✔ Decoupage glue (see page 7)
✔ Sponge applicator
✔ Tea candle

1 Wash and dry empty jars.

2 Cut tissue paper into strips and squares.

3 Use sponge applicator to apply decoupage glue to the outside of the glass jar.

6 When your design is finished, cover the entire outside of the jar with one more coat of decoupage glue.

4 Place tissue paper onto the glass.

5 Apply more decoupage glue over the top of the tissue paper to stick it down.

7 Allow the jar to dry for one hour before adding a candle.

11

Paper Mache Troll

Dragons, trolls, monsters, and more! There's no limit to what you can create with a few grocery bags and an old phone book. Create all sorts of mythical creatures, wherever your imagination takes you!

What You Need:

✓ 14 plastic grocery bags
✓ 14 rubber bands
✓ Tape (clear shipping tape or masking tape)
✓ Newspaper or old phone book cut into strips
✓ Paper mache paste (see page 6)
✓ Green yarn
✓ Acrylic paint

1 Crumple two bags together into a ball and secure the ball with two rubber bands. Repeat until you have seven balls.

2 Stack all of the balls together to form the head shape that you like. Secure the balls together with tape. We used clear shipping tape here.

3 Paper mache single strips onto the head form (see page 6). Cover the head completely with one layer and let it dry for 12 hours.

4 Paper mache more layers onto the head, one after the other, changing direction as you go until you have the smooth head shape you want. It's not necessary for layers to dry before adding another. Allow head to dry overnight.

5 To make facial features, you will use more strips of paper. Run paper through the paste and remove excess by running it through your fingers. Make a double strip by stacking one on top of the other.

6 For the eyes, fold layered strips in half lengthwise and roll up.

7 Roll or twist paper strips to form eyebrows, horns, nostrils, and teeth.

8 Press wet facial features to the face form until they stick.

9 If you want to add hair, wrap yarn around four fingers about ten times. Cut the yarn at each end of your fingers to create equal strands.

10 Carefully lay the head on its side and add a little paste to the side of the head. Place several strands of yarn in the paste and cover with a strip of pasted paper. Repeat on the other side.

11 Allow the troll to dry completely, 24–48 hours.

12 Paint the facial features first.

13 Paint the head. If you want to add spots, use the handle end of a paintbrush.

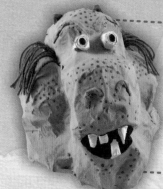

Paper Mache Treasure Box

Jazz up your desk or nightstand with a three-dimensional design you create! This trendy-looking treasure box is great for your own trinkets or perfect as a gift for Mom.

What You Need:

✓ Newspaper or old phone book

✓ Paper mache paste (see page 6)

✓ Cardboard container with lid

✓ Paint

✓ Acrylic sealer, matte finish

✓ Paintbrushes

1 Tear one or two sheets of newspaper into strips.

2 Dip a strip of newspaper into the paste and squeeze off the excess by running the paper strip through your fingers.

3 Cover your cardboard container and its lid with strips of paper, gently pressing them down with your fingers.

4 To make the heart decoration, cover three strips of paper with paste, squeezing off the excess. Layer the strips on top of one another, lining them up so they all match. Starting at one end, carefully twist the paper to create a "rope."

CLIP TIP: We made a heart, but you can make up your own decoration to top your treasure box.

5 Place the "rope" onto the lid, forming the shape of a heart. Make more "ropes" as needed to finish your design.

6 To create the rosette in the center of the lid, create a rope and coil it into a circle.

7 Allow the lid and container to dry overnight (24 hours is best).

9 Paint the raised heart and rosette in a different color.

8 Paint the outside of the container and lid in one color.

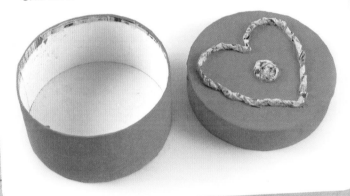

10 If you like, add simple stripes around the container.

11 After paint has dried completely, use another brush to cover with two coats of acrylic sealer. Make sure to wait 30 minutes between coats so the sealer dries.

TACK FACT

The first person to make and sell paper in the United States was Benjamin Franklin. He helped to start 18 paper mills in and around Virginia. Cotton and linen rags were used to make the paper.

STUFF TO TWIRL

Beads

What You Need:

✓ Scrapbook paper

✓ Ruler

✓ Pencil

✓ Scissors

✓ White craft glue or glue stick

✓ Toothpick

✓ Clear sealer

If you've ever wondered how to make your own paper beads, you're going to be surprised at just how easy it is! They look pretty amazing but, really, they're a breeze. So get ready to make bracelets, necklaces, and more with your very own homemade paper beads.

1 Cut scrapbook paper into strips: ½-inch wide for small beads, 1-inch wide for larger beads.

2 Turn strips over and use a ruler and pencil to draw a line from one corner to the opposite corner, creating two long, skinny triangles.

3 Use scissors to cut along the line, making two triangular strips.

4 Place a toothpick along the wide edge of the triangle. Apply glue to the triangle strip, except for ¼ inch near the toothpick. Roll the paper tight around the toothpick until completely coiled.

5 Slip out the toothpick and roll another bead. Allow glue on beads to dry. You can string the beads as they are, or if you want them to last a long time, use a paintbrush to apply clear sealer to each bead and let that dry.

CLIP TIP:
If you don't have any scrapbook paper, you can use construction paper, magazine pages, old stationery, etc. Try mixing it up!

Spinning Top

Is it raining outside? No worries! All you need are a few toothpicks and paper to make a spinning, twirling top or two. The sun will be out before you know it!

1 Cut scrapbook paper into 24 ¼-inch-wide strips.

2 Add a dot of glue to the end of the toothpick, about ¼ inch from the tip.

What You Need:

✓ Scrapbook paper
✓ Scissors or craft knife
✓ Toothpick
✓ White craft glue

3 Place the end of one of the strips into the glue and carefully wrap it around the toothpick to secure.

4 Continue wrapping the paper around the toothpick until you reach the end of the strip. Glue the end of the strip down.

5 Add another strip, beginning where the last one ended.

6 Repeat steps 4 and 5 until all strips are used, or the disk you have created measures 1¼ inches in diameter.

7 Use your index finger and thumb to gently coax the disk upward without separating the coils too far so that they come apart. Shape the disk into a cone for the top.

8 To play, hold the toothpick handle as close to the center of the top as you can and spin.

Quilled Art

Do you know what a quill is? That's right! It's a feather from a large bird that was used as a pen hundreds of years ago. The art of quilling—wrapping thin strips of paper into coils—got its name because the paper was originally wrapped around a quill. These days you can use a skewer or a dowel and make tons of cool designs!

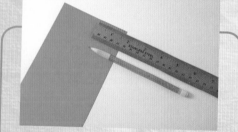

1 Mark the top and bottom of your card stock in ⅛-inch increments.

2 Place a ruler on top of the card stock, lining up the pencil marks. Using the ruler as a guide, cut strips using your craft knife.

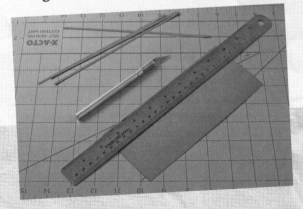

3 Use the craft knife to cut a small notch in the end of the dowel or skewer (if using a wooden skewer, trim the pointed end off).

4 Insert the end of a strip of paper into the notch. This will hold your paper in place.

5 Wrap the paper strip tightly around the dowel.

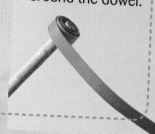

6 Release the coiled paper.

7 Use a small dab of glue to secure the open end of the coil to create a closed circle, then carefully remove your coil from the dowel.

8 Glue coils to a piece of paper to create animals, insects, flowers, cars, buildings—whatever you like! Make your coils tight or loose or turn them into leaf shapes. It's up to you!

Loose coil

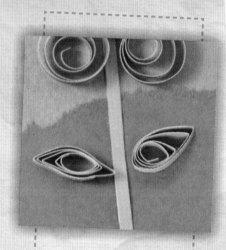

Make a leaf or tear shape by pinching one or both ends.

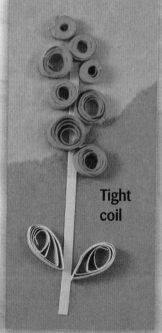

Tight coil

To make antennae only coil half of a strip.

For wings, coil both ends of a strip.

What You Need:

✓ Cardboard rolls

✓ Craft paint

✓ Scissors

✓ White craft glue

Coiled Cardboard Sculptures

You've probably sculpted things out of play dough or clay, but did you know that you could "sculpt" cardboard? Paint makes cardboard wet, which makes it soft and more pliable. Here's a fun and easy project you can try using cardboard toilet paper rolls!

1 Paint the cardboard tubes inside and out and allow them to dry to the touch. You should be able to handle them without getting wet paint on your fingers, after about 20 minutes. Don't wait too long or the paint will be too dry.

2 Starting at one end of the tube, use scissors to cut the tube into one long strip.

CLIP TIP #1: The trick is to shape the cardboard once the paint has dried enough for you to touch it. Don't wait too long or it will be stiff again!

3 Shape strip into a coil by wrapping it around your fingers or around a cylindrical object such as a small bottle of craft glue. You can also wrap the tube into a tight coil to form a disk.

4 Allow the shaped coil to dry completely, at least four hours. You want the cardboard to completely dry out so that it will stiffen up and hold its shape.

5 Turn your coil into anything you want! Add eyes or legs to make a creature. Decorate with more paint, sequins, markers, or whatever you like!

CLIP TIP #2: When cutting the cardboard tube, make the strip wider for a shorter coil, like you might use for a bracelet. Make the strips very narrow for long, coiled ceiling decorations that are great for a birthday party!

CLIP TIP #3: To make a coiled tree, create a simple cone shape from a piece of cardboard and tape it to secure it. Coil your cardboard tube strip into a disk and let it sit for about 30 minutes. Gently stretch out the coil and shape it over and onto the cardboard cone you created and let it dry completely.

HA!

Q. What is the maximum number of times a sheet of paper can be folded in half?

A. Once—after that you are folding it in quarters and then eighths, etc.!

What You Need:

✓ White paper
✓ Pencil
✓ Colored card stock paper
✓ Scissors
✓ Markers
✓ String
✓ Glue

Coiled Paper Mobile

No matter what the holiday or occasion, these easy-to-make coiled paper mobiles are a great way to decorate! Hang them from the ceiling or an entryway for a fun and festive look.

1 Use a drinking glass or other round object and trace a circle (3-4 inches in diameter) onto white paper. Cut out the circle.

2 Use a pencil to draw a spiral in the white paper circle, starting at the center.

3 Trace and cut another circle from colored card stock.

4 Hold the white circle over the top of the colored circle and cut along the spiral's lines, working from the outside toward the center.

5 Decorate your mobile with markers to create the character or design you like. You can use our ideas or make up one of your own.

6 Bend the center of the spiral upward and attach a piece of string with glue.

STUFF TO WEAVE

Weaving Basics

Weaving is an ancient art form that has been around for literally thousands of years! Your clothes, the basket that holds your toys, and even your school backpack were all made from one form of weaving or another. There are many things you can make once you know how to weave. Paper weaving is fun to do and looks great when finished! Here is an easy way to practice weaving with paper.

CLIP TIP #1: For interesting designs, when cutting the folded paper, cut different widths or cut in a zig-zag or wavy pattern.

CLIP TIP #2: Use several colors instead of just two, or vary the width of the strips you weave in.

1 Fold one piece of construction paper in half. Starting at the folded edge, cut slits every inch, stopping at about ½ inch from the edge. This is called the "warp" and the slits you just made are called "warp strips." Open the warp and lay it flat.

2 Cut the other piece of construction paper lengthwise into 1-inch-wide strips. These are called "weft strips."

3 Take one of the weft strips and insert it into the first warp strip. Thread the weft strip through the remaining warp strips in an over/under pattern.

WEFT →

WARP →

4 Take another weft strip and repeat step 3, only this time begin your weave in the opposite pattern, going under/over each warp strip.

5 Repeat steps 3 and 4 until finished.

23

What You Need:

- ✓ Scrapbook paper (two different colors or patterns)
- ✓ Scissors or a paper cutter
- ✓ Glue stick
- ✓ Large googly eye

Woven Fish

Here's another fun weaving project using folded paper strips to create a colorful fish. Use several different colors and patterns to create an entire school of these beautiful angelfish!

1 Cut scrapbook paper into six 1-inch-wide strips. We're using multicolored and yellow paper here but you can use any paper you like.

2 Fold each strip in half.

3 Place one folded strip (multicolored) on the table and insert a second folded strip (yellow) into the first. The top of the yellow strip should now be on top.

4 Add a second yellow strip. Weave it under the top and over the bottom of the multicolored strip.

5 Weave in a third yellow strip.

6 Now weave in two more multicolored strips in the other direction.

7 Tighten up all the strips so that they are all touching each other. You should see the shape of a fish begin to form.

8 Fold the middle strip of each pattern to the back and glue in place.

TACK FACT

According to Guinness World Records, the longest chain of paper dolls was created by the International School of Kabul in Afghanistan. It was over four miles long!

9 Turn the fish right side up and attach a googly eye.

Paper Plate Weaving

Weaving yarn on a disk is easy for all ages and the results can be stunning. Watch as your design comes together in this awesome project.

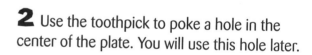

1 Cut an odd number of 1-inch slits around the outside of the plate. They should be evenly spaced but do not need to be perfect.

2 Use the toothpick to poke a hole in the center of the plate. You will use this hole later.

3 Optional: If you want, you can trim the edges of the paper plate to look like flower petals, like we did!

4 Tape a piece of yarn to the back of the plate and run the strand through one of the slits. Note: Don't tape it over the hole.

5 With your plate face-up, wrap the strand of yarn from the first slit directly across the plate to the opposite side and through that slit as well.

6 Run the yarn around the back of the plate and up through the slit next to your beginning slit. Now bring the yarn down again across the plate and to the opposite side and run it through the next open slit. Repeat until all the slits have been covered.

7 Now poke the end of the yarn from the front to the back through the hole you made earlier. Tape the yarn to the back of the plate and trim off any excess.

8 Use your second color yarn for weaving. Tie the second color to one of the center strands on the plate on the front. Trim off the excess.

9 Cut the weaving yarn to approximately 36 inches. Wrap a piece of tape around the end to keep it from fraying as you weave.

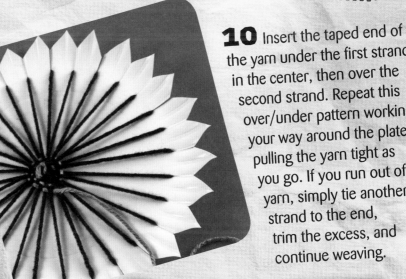

10 Insert the taped end of the yarn under the first strand in the center, then over the second strand. Repeat this over/under pattern working your way around the plate, pulling the yarn tight as you go. If you run out of yarn, simply tie another strand to the end, trim the excess, and continue weaving.

CLIP TIP:
You may want to use two paper plates together at one time if you find that one paper plate is too flimsy.

TACK FACT

Paper was invented in ancient China around 105 CE by the Han Dynasty.

Newspaper Basket

Learning how to weave your very own baskets with strips of newspaper is a little tricky at first, but you will be amazed at the results. It's really worth the effort!

1 Separate a section of newspaper into individual folded pages.

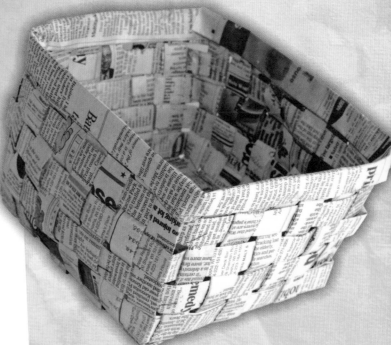

2 Cut the folded edge off each page so you have two single pages. You will need about 40 single pages to make your basket.

3 Fold a single page in half lengthwise.

4 Fold lengthwise again.

5 Open the second fold up and fold each side in toward the center crease. This will ensure there are no cut edges exposed.

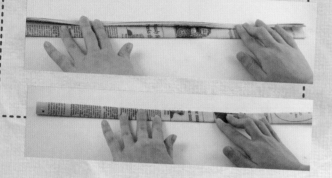

6 Repeat these steps for all 40 sheets of newspaper.

7 Place one strip on the work surface and place a second strip over the top of the first one, lining them up in the center to create a "plus sign." Now place a third strip next to the second one, only this time go under the first strip instead of over it. Place a fourth strip next to the first strip, again reversing the over/under pattern of the first.

8 Continue adding strips, horizontally and vertically, in an over/under weaving pattern. Continue weaving until you have reached a size that you want the bottom of your basket to be.

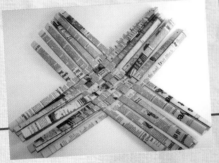

9 To create the sides of the basket, bend the excess strips upward and crease them with your fingers.

10 Weave one strip into those strips around the bottom, using a stapler to help hold them in place at each intersection as you weave.

CONTINUED →

11 Continue weaving that strip around the entire basket. If your strip is too short, you can cut another strip to fit and insert one end into the other. Secure with a stapler.

12 Weave a second strip above the first strip going over and under in the opposite pattern to the first strip.

13 Continue weaving until you reach the height that you want then trim the excess ends so that they are all the same height and flush with the top of your basket.

14 Use hot glue to cover the top edges with another strip, straddling the folded edges over each side.

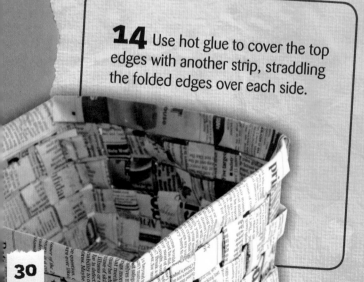

CLIP TIP: Try this project with the comics section of the paper. Or use magazine pages or wrapping paper for a more colorful basket. Try making baskets of different shapes and sizes.

Folding Basics

You've probably never thought about how many times folded paper passes through your hands. The envelopes your mail comes in, that paper airplane you tossed across the room, and what about those origami swans your uncle showed you how to make? Here are some basic folding techniques for making fabulous projects!

CREASING

Some folding projects, like origami, need to have pretty accurate folds. That's when creasing comes in handy. Creasing your paper is a way to "mark your place" so you know where you folded, especially if your project asks you to open up your folds! To get a good noticeable crease, run the back of your fingernail across the paper to make it nice and crisp.

HALF-FOLD

Folding a piece of paper in half so that it looks like a greeting card is called a half-fold or a bi-fold.

DIAGONAL FOLD

Fold a piece of paper in half diagonally, point to point.

LENGTHWISE FOLD

Fold a piece of paper in half, so the fold starts on the long edge of the paper rather than the short edge.

ACCORDION FOLD

This simple zigzag folding pattern is great for projects that have a three-dimensional look. Fold one edge of the paper and crease it. Turn the paper over. Take the first fold, which is face down, and fold it upward and crease it. Continue this pattern, flipping the paper over each time and making sure that each folded panel is the same size.

Paper Airplane

The paper airplane has been around for so many years that your grandpa's grandpa probably made one! Making one is still a great way to pass the time, especially on a rainy day! Use markers to decorate yours and send it flying.

1 Fold paper in half lengthwise and crease the center. Open the paper up again.

2 Fold the upper lefthand corner down, lining up the edge of the paper with the center crease. Repeat this for the upper righthand corner.

3 Fold the left side of the paper down toward the center of the paper again, lining up the straight edge with the center crease. Repeat on the righthand side.

4 Fold the paper along the center crease so that the left- and righthand creases are on the inside.

5 Fold the left side of the paper down, starting as close to the airplane's point as you can. Repeat for the other side.

6 Decorate with markers, take aim, and watch it fly!

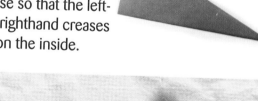

Caterpillar

Boing! These paper caterpillars are fun to make and even more fun to play with!

1 Cut four strips from each color construction paper. Each should be 2¼" x 12".

2 Tape the strips of each color together to make two long strips.

3 Place your two long strips in the shape of an "L" and tape the two ends together. We placed yellow vertically and purple horizontally.

4 Fold the yellow strip down over the purple strip.

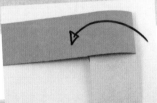

5 Fold the purple strip over across the yellow strip.

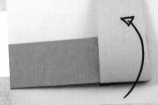

6 Fold the yellow strip up over the purple strip.

7 Keep folding until you reach the end of the strips. Use scissors to trim off any of the end strips that do not make a square.

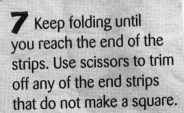

8 Glue the last flap down to the one below it. Add googly eyes, antennae (made from scraps of paper), and draw a mouth and eyebrows with a marker.

9 Boing!

Origami Star

These beautiful stars are easier to make than they look. They are awesome hanging from the ceiling for birthdays, holidays, or just for fun.

1 Fold paper in half and crease.

2 Unfold paper and fold it in half again, this time in the opposite direction.

3 Unfold paper and fold in half again, this time on a diagonal, touching corner to corner.

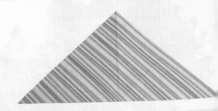

4 Unfold paper and fold in half again, on a diagonal in the opposite direction.

5 Unfold paper and place it wrong-side-up (if using double-sided paper like we did, place your favorite side down). Using a ruler and pencil, measure along each straight crease and make a mark 1¼ inches from the edge.

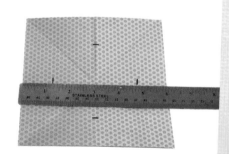

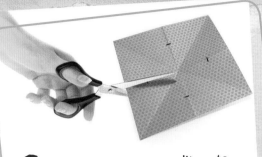

6 Use scissors to cut a slit up to each pencil mark along each crease.

7 Starting from the cut crease, fold the paper in toward the diagonal crease. Repeat this for each star point for a total of eight folds.

8 Apply glue stick to every other fold (one half of each star point).

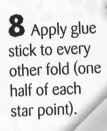

9 Slide the fold without the glue over the top of the fold with the glue and stick them together. This creates the star's points. Repeat for each point.

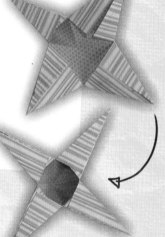

10 Follow steps 1-9 to make a second star with the other piece of paper.

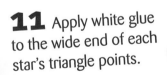

11 Apply white glue to the wide end of each star's triangle points.

12 Place the stars, back side to back side, so that they are offset, and press them together. One star should look like a "+" and the other should look like an "x."

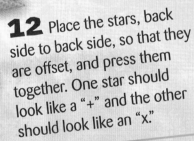

CLIP TIP: To hang the star, thread a sewing needle with thread and poke through one of the star's tips, about an inch from the top. Run the thread through and tie in a knot to create a hanger.

Paper Fan

What You Need:

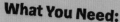

- ✓ 12" x 12" sheet of scrapbook paper
- ✓ Pencil
- ✓ 11-inch dinner plate
- ✓ 2 craft sticks
- ✓ Scissors
- ✓ Ruler
- ✓ Hot glue gun

Having a fancy tea party? Maybe you just need a pretty fan to keep you cool this summer? Whatever the reason, these fans are easy to make and you need only a few supplies!

1 Fold paper in half. Unfold and fold in half again in the opposite direction. Unfold again.

2 Place paper design-side-down and mark the center with a pencil. Place the dinner plate onto the paper. The edge of the plate should just touch the center mark.

3 Trace around the plate. Note that you can get two fans from one piece of paper if you want.

4 Cut the half circle out.

5 Place the half circle design-side-down and find the center crease. Measure up from the bottom 2¼ inches and mark with a pencil.

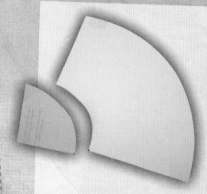

6 Fold the half circle in half, design-side in, and starting at the center mark you made in step 5, cut a curve on the bottom.

8 Starting at the point of the bottom curve, cut on a diagonal up to the ½-inch mark. Your half circle should still be folded in half so that you are cutting through two layers.

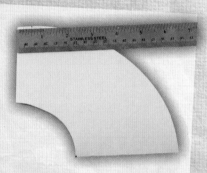

7 Measure and mark from the bottom edge of the half circle up ½ inch.

9 Open up your fan.

10 Fold accordion style in ½-inch increments, always lining up the accordion fold along the bottom curve. The accordion folds will be wider at the opposite end.

11 Open accordion and place design-side down. Use hot glue to attach a craft stick to each side, leaving an inch or so exposed at the bottom.

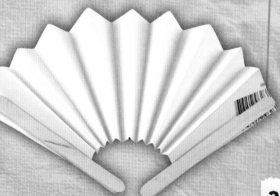

12 Finally glue the two craft sticks together at the bottom, gently stretching the fan out before the glue dries.

Fortune Cookie

Break a leg!

be great!

Happy Birthday!

Your future is clear—you are going to have a blast making these paper fortune cookies! Make one to wish someone a happy birthday, or for your parents on Mother's Day or Father's Day, or just to give your bestie a special note!

1 Cut scrapbook paper into 3½-inch-wide circles.

2 Turn the circle face down and place a glue dot near the edge.

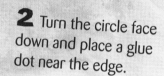

3 Fold the circle in half, securing with the glue dot. Do not crease the fold.

4 Cut the white paper into thin strips and write a message on each strip.

5 Insert the message strip into the half circle.

6 Using your forefinger in one end of the half circle, and your thumb in the other, bend the half circle backward into the shape of a fortune cookie. Secure the ends together with another glue dot.

CLIP TIP:
Use a jelly jar or plastic lid to trace your 3½-inch circle.

Make Your Own Envelope

Whether it's for a thank-you card from your birthday, or just to make your outgoing mail more colorful, a homemade envelope is easy to make and so nice to look at!

What You Need:

✓ 8½" x 11" sheet of card stock

✓ Ruler

✓ Pencil with eraser

✓ Scissors

✓ Glue stick

✓ Button or ribbon for decoration (optional)

1 Use your ruler to mark your card stock following this diagram.

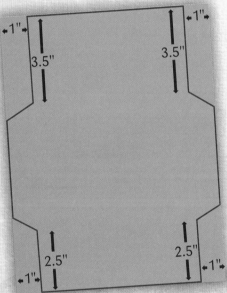

2 For each corner, cut along the vertical line until you reach the diagonal line you drew. Cut along the diagonal line as well.

3 Fold and crease the top and bottom flaps inward toward the center of the card stock. Apply glue stick to the sides of the bottom flap.

4 Fold the bottom flap upward and press onto the folded side flaps.

5 Add your letter or note and fold over the top to close your envelope. Apply glue stick to seal it shut and you are ready to deliver!

CLIP TIP:
Add some flair with a bow, a button, or another decoration!

Magazine Flower

Here's a great way to use up old magazines, wrapping paper, or just leftover construction paper. Use an accordion fold along with a fanning effect to create simple flowers that make great decorations.

1 Cut magazine page into a 4" x 6" rectangle.

2 Starting from the 4-inch end, fold accordion style until you reach the end.

3 Holding the accordion fold together, fold in half and create a crease to find the center of the stack. Staple together in the center, making sure that the staple runs in the same direction as the crease.

4 Use scissors to round both ends of the accordion fold to create the petals.

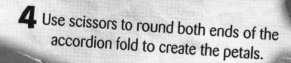

5 Apply glue stick to the top petal on one side of the staple. Fold up the sides so that the glue connects the petals together.

6 Spread the petals out to create the flower.

7 Apply glue stick on both sides of one end of a craft stick.

8 Attach the craft stick to one side of the accordion, then spread the accordion out and attach the other end.

9 Cut a circle from a magazine page for the center of the flower. Use white glue to attach it.

TACK FACT

Toilet paper dates back to the late 14th century, in China, where it was produced in 2' x 3' sheets for Chinese emperors. The toilet paper that we are familiar with today (rolled and perforated) was invented around 1880. Some sources say it was created by the Albany Perforated Wrapping Paper Company in 1877; others say it was the Scott Paper Company in 1879.

Corner Bookmark

You'll never be tempted to fold over the pages of a book to mark your place once you start making these easy and adorable bookmarks. Use fun paper, or turn them into animals. We bet your friends will be asking you to make one for them!

What You Need:

✓ 6" x 6" scrapbook paper
✓ Scissors
✓ Glue stick
✓ Paint, pens, and/or markers to decorate

1 Fold paper in half. Unfold, then fold in half again in the opposite direction, and unfold.

2 Fold paper in half diagonally, point to point. Unfold, and refold on the other diagonal.

3 Cut the paper into four triangles, cutting along the diagonals.

4 To create the tab that holds your bookmark closed, place the triangle on work surface with the top point pointing downward. Cut about ¼ inch off the top right side from the edge to the crease.

5 Now, make diagonal cuts on the corners on the left side of the triangle.

6 Refold the triangle along the crease. There will be a tab above the triangle edge.

CLIP TIP #1: To use your bookmark place it on the corner of the page in your book you wish to mark. If it seems loose you can insert several pages for a more snug fit.

CLIP TIP #2: One 6" x 6" square of scrapbook paper makes four bookmarks.

7 To seal the bookmark, apply glue stick to the tab and press it down to stick it to the triangle.

8 To make animals, use markers to create eyes, noses, whiskers, beaks, etc. You can also cut ears from additional paper and glue them on.

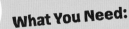

Finger Puppets

What You Need:

- ✓ Card stock
- ✓ Scissors
- ✓ White craft glue
- ✓ Googly eyes
- ✓ Markers

Oh, the possibilities! Just imagine how many different characters you could make with a little paper and some googly eyes. While there are monsters pictured here, you could make your favorite superhero or cartoon character, change the theme for each holiday, or just make goofy and silly faces.

1 Cut card stock into shapes for each character.

2 Make antennae and/or hair from strips of paper and glue to the back of each shape.

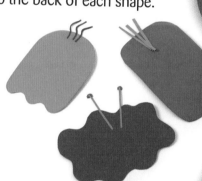

3 Cut two holes large enough for fingers to fit through.

4 Attach googly eyes with glue and let dry.

5 Insert your index and middle finger into a puppet to play.

Me Doll

Don't just make ordinary paper dolls, make a personalized "Me Doll!"

What You Need:

✓ Photo of yourself
✓ Parchment paper or tracing paper
✓ Pencil
✓ Scrapbook paper
✓ Scissors

1 Have a friend or a grown up take a picture of you wearing a tank top and shorts, a bathing suit, or a leotard. Hold your arms at your sides. Or you can wave or even pretend to be holding a bunch of balloons by clenching your fist in the air.

2 Print the photo on regular copier paper.

3 Place parchment or tracing paper over the printout and draw items of clothing such as a shirt, pants, and a skirt. Be sure to make your clothing items a little larger than the photo so that edges of your arms and legs don't show beneath the clothes.

4 Use the drawings as templates to cut out clothing items from scrapbook paper.

5 Dress up your doll using the different items, mixing and matching outfits!

CLIP TIP: Take this doll project one step further and make it magnetic! You can buy self-adhesive magnetic sheets at a craft store. Simply peel the backing off the magnet sheet and press scrapbook paper to the sheet. Then use the templates to cut out the clothes. Attach your photo to a sheet as well, and the clothing will attach and stick right to your doll!

Shadow Puppets

Just a little creativity and a lot of imagination is all you need to create great shadow puppets. Make a bird, forest animals, a princess with a dragon, a superhero—the possibilities are endless! Betcha can't wait for your next sleepover party!

What You Need:

✓ Thin cardboard (cereal box works great!)

✓ Glue stick

✓ Black construction paper

✓ Pencil

✓ White scrap paper

✓ Scissors

✓ Craft knife

✓ White craft glue or hot glue gun

✓ 12-inch wooden dowel

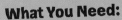

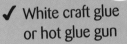

1 Cover the cardboard with glue using a glue stick and press the black construction paper over it, covering the cardboard.

2 Draw your puppet ideas on scrap paper first. Cut them out.

3 Trace around your puppet drawings on the black construction paper.

4 Cut out the puppets. With an adult's help, use a craft knife to cut out small inner pieces such as eyes and mouths.

5 Use white craft glue or hot glue to attach a dowel to the back of each puppet.

6 To have a shadow puppet show, use parchment paper or a sheet as your screen. Hang it from a tabletop and then place a lamp behind the sheet and move your puppets between the lamp and the sheet.

Marble Roadway

Building this raceway is only half the fun. When you're finished, you can spend the afternoon racing marbles down your homemade track! We've even included a marble catcher at the end so you aren't chasing marbles all over the house!

What You Need:

- ✓ Sturdy-rimmed paper plates
- ✓ Scissors
- ✓ Cardboard tubes
- ✓ Small boxes or cardboard ribbon spools
- ✓ Hot glue gun
- ✓ Parchment paper or facial tissue
- ✓ Rubber band
- ✓ Marbles

1 Cut the center out of a few paper plates. The number of plates you use totally depends on how elaborate you make your track!

2 Curve the plate rims by creasing them.

3 To create the supports for your track, use varying lengths of cardboard tubes. Use small snack or gelatin boxes, or cardboard ribbon spools, as stands for your supports.

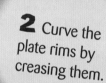

4 Hot glue tubes to stands.

5 Cut v-shaped notches in the tops of the tubes for the track to rest on.

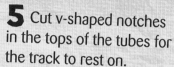

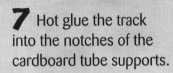

6 Assemble the track, cutting sections of plate rim and hot-gluing them together in any pattern that you like.

7 Hot glue the track into the notches of the cardboard tube supports.

8 To make your marble catcher, cut a square of parchment big enough to cover the end of a toilet paper tube (or use a piece of facial tissue). Secure it to one end of the tube with a rubber band. Place the end of the track inside the tube. No more runaway marbles!

CLIP TIP #1: Be sure to use sturdy-rimmed paper plates. The standard white plates with ridged edges will not work.

CLIP TIP #2: You may need to add guardrails wherever your marble jumps off the track. Do a test run and add 2-inch sections of plate rim along the edges of the track to keep the marble from flying off.

TACK FACT

Paper was first used as money by the Song Dynasty in China in 960 CE. Paper notes were printed with pictures of houses, trees, or people in red and black ink, and stamped with a special mark to prevent counterfeiting.

Blow Rocket

These rockets are such a blast to play with and so simple to make! Make a bunch, decorate them, and have rocket races!

What You Need:

✓ 8½" x 11" sheet of white printer/copier paper

✓ Scissors

✓ Clear tape

✓ Envelope

✓ White craft glue

✓ Tissue paper

✓ 2 drinking straws

1 Fold paper in half. Unfold, then fold in half again in the opposite direction and unfold.

2 Now you have four sections. Cut on the creases until you have four equal-sized pieces of paper.

3 Take one of the pieces of paper, and starting at the shorter side of the paper, roll it up into a tube with about a 1-inch diameter and secure it with tape.

4 Cut off the corner of an envelope; this will be the top of your rocket.

48

5 Stand the tube on end and line the top with white glue.

6 Open the envelope corner and place it on top of the tube and press it down into the glue. Allow it to dry for about 10 minutes.

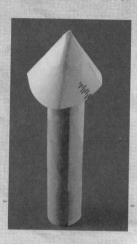

7 Cut tissue paper into thin strips about four inches long.

8 Pipe a little glue around the bottom of the tube and attach tissue paper strips.

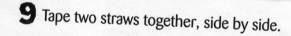

9 Tape two straws together, side by side.

10 Insert straws inside the rocket, aim, and blow!

CLIP TIP: You can make four rockets from one sheet of paper!

TACK FACT

According to Guinness World Records, the farthest flight by a paper airplane was 226 feet, 10 inches. The record was set by Joe Ayoob and aircraft designer John M. Collins at McClellan Air Force Base, North Highlands, California, in February 2012.

What You Need:

✓ Brown paper grocery bag

✓ Scissors

✓ Paint

✓ Markers, yarn for stitching, etc.

✓ Hot glue gun

✓ Plastic grocery bag or toilet paper

✓ Dowel or ruler to help with stuffing

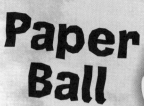

Paper Ball

Play ball! Or at least, make ball! This fun, simple project will give you all kinds of ideas for other things you can make using the same steps. Create your own stuffed animals, dolls, ornaments…the possibilities are endless!

1 Cut the bottom out of a paper bag and cut along side creases to create simple "sheets." Draw your shape on one sheet.

2 Place two sheets together and cut out the shape, cutting through both sheets, to create two cut-outs.

3 Paint shapes in desired colors.

4 Decorate shapes with markers or paint. If you want to add stitches, like we did, an adult can help you poke the sewing holes first with a regular stickpin or sewing needle. Then you can use a plastic needle and yarn to add your stitches.

5 Place decorated shapes together so that they line up evenly and hot glue the inside edges, leaving a 3-inch-wide open pocket for stuffing.

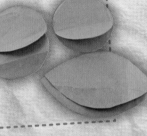

6 Now it's time to stuff. Carefully stuff a bag, or pieces of toilet paper, into the opening. It helps to use a dowel or ruler to reach into the corners.

7 Seal the opening with hot glue.

What You Need:

- ✓ Recycled cardboard boxes
- ✓ Cardboard tubes
- ✓ Construction paper
- ✓ Scissors
- ✓ Glue
- ✓ Toothpicks
- ✓ Tape

Castle

All you need to make this castle is construction paper, recycled boxes, and recycled cardboard tubes. Oh, and of course a little imagination! Why stop at just a castle? You could make an entire kingdom!

1 Cover boxes and cardboard tubes with construction paper. Secure with tape.

2 Make windows, doors, and turret and tower tops from additional construction paper.

3 Make flags from construction paper and attach them to toothpicks with tape.

4 When you are done decorating, put all the castle pieces together using glue or tape.

What You Need:

- ✓ Sturdy paper plate
- ✓ Hole puncher
- ✓ Scissors
- ✓ Plastic birthday banner, tablecloth, or garbage bag
- ✓ 20-inch wooden dowel
- ✓ Hot glue gun
- ✓ Tape

Paper Plate Kite

There's more than one way to fly a kite! You can fly this one indoors or out and it doesn't even require wind. Just hold the stick high in the air, and go!

1 Use the hole puncher to create holes halfway around the rim of the plate, about two inches apart.

2 Cut out the center circle of the plate.

3 Cut plastic into strips.

4 Insert one strip into one of the holes on the paper plate and tie in a knot. Repeat for all remaining holes.

5 Use hole puncher to poke one more hole in the plate, opposite the streamers. Gently push the dowel into the hole, twisting back and forth to work it in, being careful not to rip it.

6 Remove the dowel and tape over the hole on the bottom side of the plate.

7 Add a generous amount of hot glue over the hole and press the dowel into it, holding the dowel steady as the glue dries.

Grandpa's Newspaper Hat

What You Need:
✓ 1 large newspaper page

Here's a project that has been around since your grandparents were kids! You can make simple hats from a page of the newspaper in just a couple of minutes.

1 Fold the newspaper on the crease. The folded end should be at the top.

2 Now fold it from left to right, like a book, and crease it. Open it up again.

3 Fold the upper left corner down until it meets the center crease. Repeat for the right side as well.

4 To make the brim of the hat, fold one sheet from the bottom upward.

5 Turn the hat over to the other side and repeat step 4.

6 If your newspaper was very long, you may want to repeat steps 4 and 5 and fold each side up again.

TACK FACT

The average household throws away 13,000 separate pieces of paper each year. (Most is packaging and junk mail!)

Fancy Hat

You will be ready for the races when you are sporting your new fancy hat! Get creative by trying different types of paper or try using real or silk flowers to decorate it. Don't forget to smile!

1 Have a grown-up or friend place the center of the newspaper on top of your head. Wrap masking tape around where the hatband should go.

2 Trim the outside of the newspaper to form a brim. If you want your final hat to look like newspaper, you can roll the brim and secure with glue and decorate. Or you can go on to the next step to cover it with tissue paper.

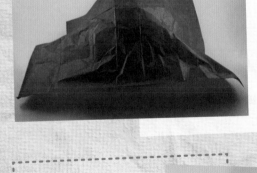

3 Place one full sheet of tissue paper on top of the hat.

4 Place a second full sheet of tissue paper on top of the hat in the opposite direction.

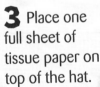

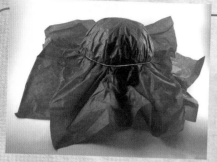

5 To secure the tissue paper, wrap a rubber band around the tissue paper where the hat band would be.

6 Turn the hat upside down and fold the tissue paper onto the newspaper brim and secure with tape or glue.

7 To make a hatband, take another sheet of tissue paper in a contrasting color and fold it in half corner to corner. Roll it up and twist it to make a "rope." Glue the rope onto the hat brim, covering the rubber band.

8 Decorate with tissue paper flowers (see page 56).

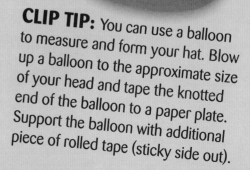

CLIP TIP: You can use a balloon to measure and form your hat. Blow up a balloon to the approximate size of your head and tape the knotted end of the balloon to a paper plate. Support the balloon with additional piece of rolled tape (sticky side out).

Tissue Paper Flowers

1 Cut tissue paper into 6-inch squares.

2 Line up two squares together evenly. Fold up accordion style (see page 31).

(see page 31).

What You Need:

✓ Tissue paper

✓ Scissors

✓ Yarn

3 Trim both ends of the folded tissue paper to make rounded or pointed petals.

4 Fold in half to find the center then tie the center with a piece of yarn. Trim excess yarn.

5 Fan out the tissue paper.

CLIP TIP: Once you know how to make tissue paper flowers, you will find all kinds of uses for them. Add pipe cleaner stems and make a bouquet!

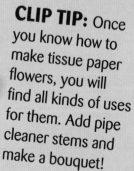

6 Carefully pull the layers apart and arrange until you are happy with the look.

Paper Doily Crown

Make a beautiful crown fit for a princess using a paper doily. We used colored pencils to decorate ours, but markers or craft paint will work great, too!

What You Need:

✓ 10-inch round paper doily

✓ 1 sheet white copier paper

✓ Scissors

✓ Tape

✓ Colored pencils, markers, or paint

✓ Stapler

1 Fold doily in half.

2 Cut paper in half lengthwise.

3 Fold each half into thirds.

4 Tape the paper strips to the left and right side of the doily.

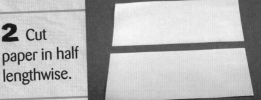

5 Turn it over and tape the strips to the front of the doily, too.

6 Decorate with colored pencils, markers, or paint.

7 Have someone help fit the crown around your head. Staple together at the back and trim excess paper. Cover the staples with tape.

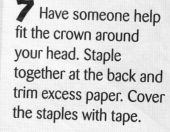

57

Photo Booth Props

Making props to use while taking pictures with your friends is loads of fun! Use classic props, like mustaches and eyeglasses, or get wacky with googly eyes and funny smiles! These are great for a birthday party, and if there's a theme make props to go with it and have a blast clicking pics.

What You Need:

- ✔ Posterboard in various colors
- ✔ Pencil
- ✔ Scissors
- ✔ Dowels in varying lengths, starting at 12 inches
- ✔ Hot glue gun

1 Use a pencil to draw your prop shapes onto the posterboard.

2 Cut out props with scissors.

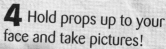

3 Hot glue dowels to the back of the props.

4 Hold props up to your face and take pictures!

CLIP TIP: These work great for selfies, too!

Paper Bag Costumes

Need a costume for a school play? Can't come up with an idea for Halloween? Grab a paper bag! Be creative and think outside the box, or should we say, think outside the bag? We bet you can come up with plenty of ideas! Here are some to get you started…

CAT HEAD

1 Spray bag with orange spray paint.

2 Cut orange triangles from construction paper and smaller pink triangles. Glue the pink triangles to the orange triangles. Glue to the top of the mask.

3 Cut a large pink triangle with rounded corners for the nose. Glue to the front of the mask.

4 Cut three black pipe cleaners in half and glue three to each side of the mask as whiskers.

5 Use a black marker to draw stripes, eyes, and mouth.

6 Try the mask on then mark and cut eye holes so you can see!

ROBOT

1 Spray bag with silver spray paint.

2 Make light panels, buttons, and knobs from construction paper, and glue to the bag.

3 Use a black marker to add detail.

4 Cut holes for your arms and your head.

CONTINUED →

FISHERMAN

1 Cut bag down the center on one side to make a vest. Cut arm holes.

2 Glue on construction paper pockets.

3 Use markers to draw hooks and lures.

4 Make a bobber and additional lures from construction paper and attach to vest.

5 Wear vest and a floppy fishing hat, and carry a fishing pole.

CLOWN

1 Spray bag with light-colored spray paint.

2 Add polka dots with craft paint and a round applicator sponge.

3 Cut a piece of construction paper in half lengthwise for the collar. Glue to the bag. To decorate collar, glue pom-poms to the edge.

4 Make paper pom-poms for the front of the clown outfit by cutting a piece of construction paper into three 3-inch-wide strips. Follow folding instructions for magazine flowers on pages 40, only don't trim the ends, leave them as is. Glue these to the front of the costume.

5 Cut holes for your arms and your head.

FLOWERY DRESS OR TOP

1 Spray bag with light-colored spray paint.

2 Use acrylic craft paint and a round applicator sponge to make flowers all over the dress.

3 Fringe the bottom by cutting slits in the opening of the bag.

4 Cut holes for your arms and your head.

SHERIFF

1 Cut bag down the center on one side to make a vest. Cut arm holes.

2 Glue on construction paper pockets.

3 Make a star from cardboard.

4 Cover it with silver duct tape or aluminum foil. Glue the star to the vest.

5 Glue buttons on to the pockets and down the center of the vest.

MONSTER HEAD

1 Spray paint bag with a bright color.

2 Cut eye from construction paper. Make a large circle from white, a medium circle from green, and a smaller circle from black. Glue to the bag.

3 Cut a tooth from white paper and glue to the bag.

4 Use a black marker to add an eyebrow and a mouth.

5 Try mask on, then mark and cut eye holes so you can see!

STUFF TO CREATE

Making Paper

Paper—it's everywhere. But did you know you could make your own paper? It's pretty easy and fun, too! Once your paper is dry, you can cut it into notebooks or use it in scrapbook projects!

1 Use four of the stir sticks to form a rectangle or a square. Glue them together to make a frame.

2 Cover the entire frame with cheesecloth. Hot glue another stick on top of the cheesecloth at one end, sandwiching the cheesecloth inside the frame.

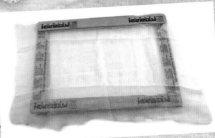

3 Glue on the remaining three sticks, carefully stretching the cheesecloth as you go. You want the cheesecloth to be stretched tight. Trim extra cheesecloth. Now your frame is ready!

4 Tear your paper into squares. Fill the blender container halfway with the paper pieces.

5 Fill blender container with warm water.

6 Blend on low for 10-15 seconds then increase speed as the paper begins to breaks up. There should be no chunks of paper left after about 30-40 seconds.

7 Put your frame into your basin and pour the mushed up paper (pulp) over the frame. Lift the frame, allowing the excess water to drip off. Gently press the pulp with your hands to release more water.

8 Move the frame to a towel. Fold towel over to cover frame. Press on the towel over the frame to release as much water from the pulp as you can. You may need to move the frame to a dry section of the towel and start again. Keep at it until it's really hard to get any more water to come out.

CLIP TIP #1: We used torn up toilet paper for our photos, but you can use other types of paper for different results. You can even add things like seeds, flower petals, or glitter.

CLIP TIP #2: If you don't want to make a frame out of paint sticks, you can use an old picture frame.

CLIP TIP #3: You can use an old piece of screen instead of cheesecloth.

9 To remove the paper from the screen, turn it upside down and carefully peel it off. Transfer to a safe place to dry completely.

Paper Tricks

WALK THROUGH A PIECE OF PAPER

Here's a great trick to amaze your friends. Hold up a plain piece of copier paper and tell them that you are going to walk right through it. "No way!" they will say.

Well, here comes the tricky part. Fold the paper in half lengthwise and cut slits following the diagram below. Be sure to cut at the fold between the red arrows as well. Then unfold the paper, pull it apart and presto! There will be an opening, big enough for you to walk through!

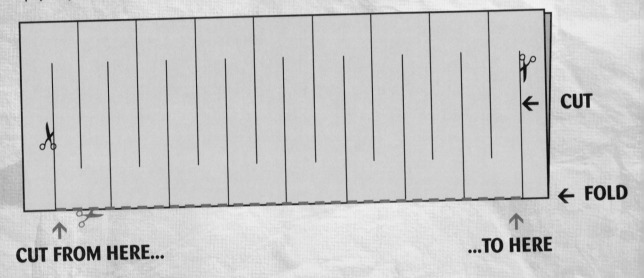

← CUT

← FOLD

CUT FROM HERE...   ...TO HERE

FOLD IT UP

This one really isn't a trick, but it's pretty awesome. Take a piece of paper, any size, and fold it in half. Fold it in half again. And again. And again. How many times can you fold it before it's too hard to fold again?

Here's the awesome part—no matter what size paper you start with, you will never be able to fold it more than seven times. Try it!

MAGIC CIRCLE

Make a loop out of a strip of paper and cut it in half. Your friends will be expecting you to end up with two loops, but you will have one really big loop!

Here's what you do: Cut a strip of paper from a piece of copier paper. Twist the paper once and tape it to make a loop*.

Cut the loop down the center of the strip all the way around. Say some magic words and open it up. You will have one big loop! Voila!

*This kind of loop is a called a Mobiüs loop.

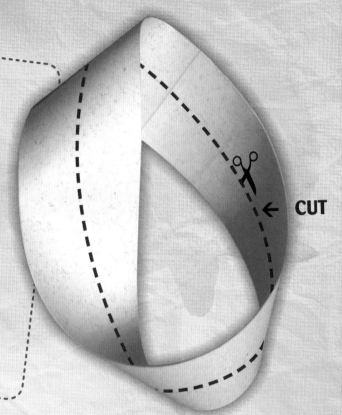

CUT

THE AMAZING FLOATING PAPER CLIP

Want to amaze your friends? Challenge them to make a paper clip float in a cup of water. The paper clip will fall right to the bottom of the cup.

Now you will show them the secret. Tear off a piece of paper towel (larger than the paper clip) and place it on top of the water. Put the paper clip on the paper towel and wait a few seconds. The towel will sink to the bottom, but the clip will stay floating on top!

Magic? Your friends will think so, but it's actually a scientific property called surface tension that allows the clip to float. The surface tension of the water keeps the paper floating. As the paper towel sinks, it lowers the paper clip into the water without breaking the surface tension.

Wrapping Paper

Out of wrapping paper? Head over to the store and grab yourself a roll of brown "kraft" paper and some bubble wrap and make your own colorful paper for wrapping up gifts!

What You Need:

✓ Scissors
✓ Bubble wrap
✓ Paint
✓ Paintbrush
✓ Brown kraft paper

1 Cut bubble wrap into squares that will fit into the palm of your hand, about four inches wide.

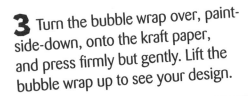

2 Use a paintbrush to paint simple designs onto the bumpy side of the bubble wrap.

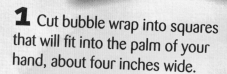

3 Turn the bubble wrap over, paint-side-down, onto the kraft paper, and press firmly but gently. Lift the bubble wrap up to see your design.

4 Decorate your paper with any designs and colors that you like and let it dry before using as wrapping paper.

CLIP TIP: The marbled paper on page 70 is great for wrapping up gifts, too!

Secret Writing

Write a secret message that no one can see, then reveal it like magic with some watercolor paint. What a fun thank-you note this could be for a birthday party: Send your guests home with a "blank" note and a new pack of watercolor paints.

1 Use a white crayon to write a message onto a white piece of paper.

2 Paint over the crayon with watercolor paint to reveal the secret message!

CLIP TIP #1: You can use this same technique for drawing secret pictures, too!

CLIP TIP #2: You can also write a secret message on a piece of paper using lemon juice. After it dries, hold the paper up to a standard lightbulb to reveal the message!

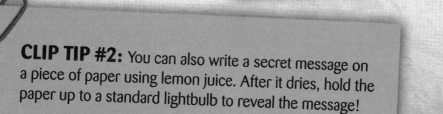

Scratch Paper

You may have tried this in art class—art teachers love it! If you haven't tried it yet, it might feel a little strange painting your artwork completely black, but we promise you will love the results!

What You Need:

- ✓ White card stock or heavy white paper
- ✓ Crayons in bright colors
- ✓ Black acrylic or poster paint
- ✓ Paintbrush
- ✓ Wooden skewer, toothpick, or craft stick

1 Color the paper in sections using bright and colorful crayons. You will need to fill in the entire surface—do not leave any white areas.

2 Paint the entire surface of your colored cardstock with black paint. You should not be able to see any color beneath the paint. If you do, add another coat.

3 Allow the paint to dry completely, about two hours.

4 Use a skewer to draw on the paint surface. This will scratch off the paint, revealing the beautiful colors beneath it.

TACK FACT

The average American family uses seven trees worth of paper every year!

Flip Book

Flip books are easy to make and you will be amazed at how your simple drawings come to life when you flip through the pages.

What You Need:

✓ 4 sheets white copier paper

✓ Paper cutter or scissors

✓ Stapler

✓ Fine-point pen

1 First you make your book. Stack the four sheets of paper evenly so they all match up. Use the paper cutter to cut the sheets in half. (You can use scissors if you don't have a paper cutter.)

2 Take each of those stacks and cut them in half again. Take those stacks and cut each of them in half once more.

3 Staple all of the stacks together across the top (the narrow end).

4 Now it's time to draw! Draw a simple picture at the bottom corner of the first page.

5 Go to the next page and draw a similar picture, only change it a little.

6 Keep drawing a slightly different image on each page until you've reached the end of the pad.

7 Hold the bottom of the pad with your fingers at the back and thumb in front. Flip the pages, releasing one at a time through your thumb to watch your animation!

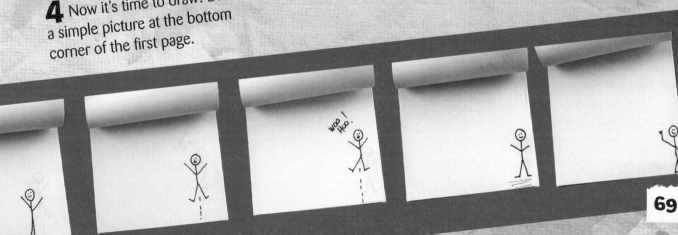

Marbled Paper

Spend an afternoon making beautiful marbled designs on paper. Then fold the paper to make your own homemade stationery or note cards. Or use it to cover a book or wrap a present. There are many ways to marble paper; we are using shaving cream!

1 Fill one of the baking sheets with shaving cream. You can cover the tray with aluminum foil first for easier cleanup.

2 Spread the shaving cream smooth with a ruler or paint stirrer then add drops of paint across the top.

3 Drizzle more paint onto the shaving cream.

4 Use a toothpick to swirl the paint around.

5 Place a sheet of paper on top of the shaving cream and using circular motions, gently press the paper into the shaving cream.

6 Carefully lift a corner of the paper and peel it off of the shaving cream.

7 Place the design shaving-cream-side-up on the second baking sheet.

8 Use your ruler to squeegee off the shaving cream, leaving the paint design behind. Place paper aside to dry.

CLIP TIP #1: You can create a starburst design by adding drops of paint and dragging the toothpick through the drops in different directions to make stars.

CLIP TIP #2: Try using food coloring instead of craft paint.

Amanda Formaro is a Midwest mother of four who has been creating crafts for kids for over 20 years. She has been published in several major magazines and websites, including *Parents*, *Redbook*, and *Family Fun*, and websites including Family.com, and Spoonful.com. Her passion for crafting resonates in her blog, **CraftsbyAmanda.com**, where she shares tutorials with step-by-step photos for adults and kids alike. Amanda loves the creative process and trying new things, and especially likes making something from nothing.